Disclaimer

Sowing the seeds

This e-book is written for informational purposes only. Who

Efforts have been made to make this e-book as complete as possible

as accurately as possible. However, it may contain errors

typography or content. Furthermore, this e-book

contains information only

until the release date. Therefore, this e-book should be used

as a guide - not as a definitive source.

The purpose of this e-book is to educate. Author and

the publisher does not warrant that the information contained herein

The e-book is completely prepared and is not responsible for anything

errors or omissions. Author and publisher cannot have both

liability or responsibility to any person or entity

loss or damage caused or alleged to be caused directly or

indirectly through this e-book.

Content

Introduction

There is probably no one who has not heard the expression "sow seeds".

in one form or another. The expression "what you sew, you cut" is common.

also, but how does it work in business?

Think of it in gardening. You plant a seed, you feed it, it grows,

and be paid for the finished product. Business is hard work

a seed You use dedication, time and hard work and grow a

a quality business that you can profit from.

Likewise, a business cannot grow without planting and nurturing seeds.

Without the hard work required to grow your business

can't wait to be rewarded. Sometimes even the smallest action can

you can win big prizes. But idleness does not give up

awards in other words, do nothing, get nothing.

You can spend half your life building a business. This can be your most

considerable property. The success of this company could weaken the economy

the future of your family. Plan your business and build what you need

seeds lay the foundation for the success of your business. take care of it

and it can grow into a business that will bring you great benefits.

What seeds should you plant for success?

For your business to be successful, it is not just

It is important to plant seeds, but plant the right seeds. Any farmer will tell you

you know that certain seeds do not grow in certain areas of the world. What blooms in one region fades in another. Here are some real ones

the seeds you need to plant for your business to succeed:

• Submit valuable keyword content to your blog

Obviously, everything you post on your blog should be

valuable Readers simply don't want to read it otherwise. That's it

the phrase "Think before you speak" applies. In other words,

"Think before you blog." Think about the important, the valuable information you can convey and communicate to your reader a

in a way that draws them in and makes them want to read on

what will you say next

The second part of this seed is a bit more complicated. you

may contain the most valuable content on the Internet, but if not

if anyone sees it, it won't do you any good. So

You want to use keyword-targeted content to make sure they work

your blog posts.

Companies have been using keyword-targeted ads for a long time

time, but many don't realize how important it can be to a blog content Because search engines pick up on these words and

getting your blog to appear in searches can be a valuable tool

increase website traffic. However, you are not just garbage

your content in a few words and hope they notice

search engines You can ensure a few steps

you get the right keywords.

1. Keyword Research - Find out how many people

looking for your site. The tools are available at

Google and other developers who can help

the process will be easier for you.

2. Target low competition, niche keywords - Google

Adwords can be very useful to see how competitive a

keyword is before you decide to use it.

3. Don't just focus on the most important keywords - try to think

out of the box Keyword targeting isn't just about that

most popular keywords. For example, if you are a real estate agent,

just targeting your blog real estate will bring you too much

even catches attention. Aim for a specific reality

instead of real estate and get other visitors to your site

property only targeting is not allowed.

4. Think about what your target market is looking for and put it there

it on your website. Always think about your market first. They

you want quality content, not keywords. If you have

with quality content, you should write 200-300

content words for each keyword used. About that

three to five keywords on each page. Don't force it

that. Keywords should be used naturally to flow

within the content

5. Change the titles and descriptions of each page - Search

engines don't understand what your topic is

importance of each page if you use the same tags for all

pages

6. Prepare a site map showing where everything is

web - search engines such as sitemaps. Even if you can

around 1% CTR, sitemap really helps

who know what to do with them.

7. Increase Popularity - Doing the above will not help

you on the first pages of the search pages. to do

you have to build popularity. One way is to reach out

websites that link to yours. You can provide an important

information so that others will want to link to your site. If you

don't spam and have a well linked site you will do better

search engines

After you have written your valuable content and posted it

targeted keywords, you can use other places

also, keywords:

1. URL - Using keywords means more in the root domain

than subdomains, but good root domains often are

hard to reach Try to add at least one keyword

root domain if you cannot use the full phrase. if not,

however, putting it on a subdomain will help you rank higher.

2. Page Titles – Page titles are great for search

engine arrangements Use every keyword in the title

page, especially at the beginning of a page title, will

help with ranking.

3. Inbound links using anchor text - this is a section

the text of the clickable link. If your anchor text is

with a targeted keyword, it will improve the ranking of the keyword.

4. Title - Titled texts, such as page titles, have more impact

keyword rank than content. Takes one part

A title that includes the keyword is to your advantage.

5. Bold text - Bold text stands out on the page, but also

stand out as a keyword in search rankings.

6. Image ALT text - Search engines don't read images, but

you can put keyword-based ALT text on images. It will come

helps determine page rank. Found for some sites

can be valuable in image search.

These are just a few suggestions, but they are valuable.

Using the right keywords on your blog is essential

its growth.

Now that you understand the meaning of the keyword

optimization, it might be time to reevaluate some old ones

content You may find valuable content that you need

modified and reused with keywords. Many old

the blogs you post are like seeds planted in stone

to the soil, can be transplanted with the right keywords and can

to bloom Doing this is easier than it seems. Everything you need is here

do:

1.See analytics and find your most popular posts.

2. Read them and think about how you could summarize them

using only three to four words.

3. Once you've got a blog topic figured out, look for what

people are searching on Google—You can use Google's

Keyword Tool, put in your description, and Google will do

the rest. It will give you the results for your phrases and

for similar phrases.

4. Look for keywords that have low/medium competition. This will help you understand these words better.

5. Check the sentences and make sure they are on target

the audience you want to target.

6. Optimize your blog posts - use keywords

developed and put them in your blog post. Confirm

save content in a readable format.

7. Use the best keyword or phrase in your title.

• Systematization - recording and documentation of processes

No two organizations are exactly alike. Your method

work differentiates you from your competitors and

makes you stand out as unique. Often business

methods are brought by the people working in the company.

What worked for them before did.

It's all good when it works, but it can be difficult

tell the new employee the secret formula.

I'm trying to figure out how something should work after that

it went wrong, it should work. If you have

well thought out plan and document your strategy and so it goes

it is easy for staff to diagnose the problem and help prevent it

of recurring problems. This will help you avoid doing the same thing

critical errors.

When starting a business, you can experiment

to do different things. If you document each

process, you'll see what works best. It gives you a chance

improve the process and make the company run better

effectively. Then a well-documented process can also be helpful

someone important leaves the company unexpectedly. It could be

so that the new employee can handle all his tasks

new job

Very few love docs. Your documentation

business processes don't actually add revenue to your top line. If

You focus on being efficient with the money you have, you can do it

add value to your business and help it grow.

Once you have created appropriate documentation for each of your tasks

you can delegate these tasks to your employees

you order by outsourcing.

• Create valuable eBooks to sell or giveaway

Creating your own information products is a great way to get

passive income and traffic. You create it once and get paid over

and over for the one-time effort you put into it.

Selling informational products really comes down to marketing.

From the topic, to how you plan to sell it depends on what

people want to buy willing to pay for.

The great thing about ebooks is that they don't have to be as

long as regular books. People often buy e-books that are

anywhere from 10 to 50 pages when they solve a problem that people

want a solution

You're probably thinking, "Why should people pay for anything

can they get it for free if they look for it online?" Many people

you don't want to or don't have time to do a thorough investigation. They

can also be a bit skeptical about open sources. If you confess

you are trusted or perhaps partnered with someone who is

and if you solve a problem, people will want to buy yours

a book Writing about what you love may not be what's next

for sale Write down what the customer wants to buy and you will.

Here are some tips to help you create even more

profit from the sale of electronic books:

☐ Sell or sell e-books monthly updates

never issued for further profit.

☐ Give free ebooks along with paid ebooks. It often does

it's okay to let others give away your free e-book as well.

☐ Separate your e-book into several reports and give to people

buy only the data they want. ☐ Purchase reprint rights for other e-books. Add them to yours

to the packing contract.

☐ Add links to your ad text. The way people click

this will take them to the order page.

☐ Sell half of your book cheap and give it to them

option to buy the whole book at full price if they like it.

☐ Offer free, related material to the books you're selling.

☐ Give a sample page with important info blacked out.

It

may make your prospective customers curious enough to

buy it.

☐ Give both low and high-priced copies of your books.

Show people the contents of each so they can compare

them, and usually, they'll pay for the extra information.

☐ Offer reprint rights for electronic purchase.

You can sell them at a higher price than usual

purchase price

Keep your eBook format accessible to people offline.

This can be an audiobook, a video or a printed copy.

☐ Look at specific niches and redesign your book to fit

these niches.

☐ Offer discount coupons to shoppers

your e-book for other products. It can be your product or

someone you contracted with.

☐ Pay for recurring monthly subscriptions by splitting your subscription in half

e-books for online newsletter questions.

As you can see, e-books can be quite profitable

business in many different ways and they are definitely worth doing

time to write

• Network and build relationships with other experts in your field

chassis

Relationships are important to any business. Many people know this

getting to know people in your field should just happen

for competitive reasons. Network with other experts in your field can be very useful to you for other reasons as well. You never know, one day you might make a joint venture and create a

product together or even share ideas worth millions.

People enjoy interacting with each other. it is

why creating networks in a different form was necessary

a tool for business survival for hundreds of years. It can

to be positive for you and bring successful results to many

why and wherefore:

1. Opportunity - You have the opportunity to meet new people every time

when you leave home. You never know what kind of people you are

or what that person may have. Perspective

it's everywhere if you take the chance. Take the positive

look around, see what's out there and start networking

with others. You have nothing to lose by trying.

2. Exhibition - Get yourself, your talent or your business out there

there" requires exposition. You can be a new musician

you've just created a great new product or you're struggling to get yours

business in progress. Anyway, the more people you know, the better

you feel better Your customers or fans are talking to each other

himself They can also chat with people outside the social circle

you are inside. You may already have fans or customers, but

remember more is better.

3. Contacts/Relationships - I'm sure you've heard the old saying,

"It's not what you know, but who you know." That's what

makes networking VERY important. The more you connect

and the more relationships you build, the more people you get

the greater the chance of meeting the right person.

You never know what "right" person you will need in the future. At first, make as many connections as possible.

Stay in touch with them and you'll be in good company

people from which to draw future needs.

4. Share common things - like-minded people enjoy each other

another company. If you have something in common

with someone, the conversation is easier and they want to build a

relationship with you Communities connect people,

and can tie them together.

5. Learning from each other - Networking with others certainly does this

means that information and ideas are shared. It is

there is a good chance that you will meet someone with a new idea

or vision that you feel will benefit your business. Knowing who

it's important to seek help when you need it. When it comes

knowing the right person... knowledge is power!

Networks go hand in hand with successful operations

business However, many of us are seriously afraid of walking a

fend off strangers and introduce yourself. These

event types are however important and if you know you have

to do them, do better if you are positive about them

attitude Here are some tips to help you.

1. Don't be late - I know it's tempting to show up

at the last moment and sneaks into the back of the room, but does not

do the work on the other hand, the early appearance of will

to give you a good start. If you do, you will find it

people are quieter and calmer than when the event is full

swing People haven't split into groups yet, so it is what it is

much easier to find people to talk to. If you are a small an an introvert, it's easy to become a wallflower at these events when

you are not careful. Early emergence reduces stress and

helps you make valuable connections.

2. Ask simple questions - if you're just waiting on the road

a space where people can come and talk to you, but they can't. You can do it

seem unapproachable or unwilling to talk to others.

Instead, start the conversation with simple questions. go

to an individual or group of people and simply ask, "Can I

join you?" They're also there to meet new people, so that's what they do

be glad to be a member of their group. Ask questions, e.g.

"What brings you to this event?" These are simple questions

that breaks the ice and starts a conversation. find

that by doing so the conversation is easy. You are inside

same company so you already have things in common.

Remember the second part of the conversation,

but... listening. If you're more of an introvert, you are

probably a good listener. Listen carefully to their answers.

Listening is a very good way to meet new people and

pick a few key ideas you might want to use

business

3. Check the sales pitch at the door - it's not about networking

sales, it's all about building relationships. That's why you

you should leave the sales area at home or inspect it yourself

coat on the door. Nothing turns people off more

trying to sell hard in the first few minutes of the match

someone When you start a conversation, keep it light,

fun and informal. The goal is simply to start conversations

started off friendly. When people enjoy your company,

they want to do business or partner with you,

so be pleasant not overbearing.

Eventually, the conversation can turn to business.

When a potential client or business partner asks you

whatever product or service you offer, just get it

a simple description of your business. do that

make a mental list of recent accomplishments. It can be a

a new client or a great new project

you just finished Once you have them ready, you can easily do this

bring them out during the conversation when prompted.

4. Be Enthusiastic – It's easy to be enthusiastic when sharing

your passion People can't help but be excited when they are

to hear how excited, you are about your products or services.

There is definitely a good story about why you felt that way

passionate about building your own business. Share it

people You notice the tension you often feel

contagious You share your passion and others want to

share yours. It gives all participants a great,

memorable conversations and really keep you going

great time

5. Keep a smile on your face - people want to talk friendly

people and a smile give others that impression

you are such a person. Smiling is so easy, but people

usually forget its importance. Even if you seriously DON'T

If you want to be there, you will find that a smile makes you feel better

state of mind Have a negative attitude, and replace it

a simple smile and you start to feel the difference right

outside Start smiling before you walk into the room and you can do it

make instant impressions that can go far.

6. Don't dominate the conversation - often, especially if

we are nervous, we tend to talk too much. If you don't want to

present, you are introverted and conversations are difficult

it's easy for you to overcompensate by controlling

discussions Remember, it's all about being a good networker

relationships One sure way to succeed in networking

is to make others feel special. If you want to do it, you want to do it

for example, making eye contact, using the person's name

into the conversation, sincerely listen to what they have to say, and

highlight easy topics to talk about. There is more to the discussion

likes to talk so be a good conversationalist...just not a big one speaker It is possible that this person does not want to be there

either. Making them easier will help you feel more comfortable.

7. Don't forget to follow up - Remember networking is

where the conversation begins. It doesn't end there.

Sometimes you meet someone, have a good conversation

with them and never hear from them again. When you meet

someone and you really hit it off, be sure to ask how

keep in touch with them. Don't leave without getting them

phone number, email address or social networks where you can be contacted

through them. Don't wait until you need that person. To enter

contact them within 48 hours. Signal

something you discussed at the event for them to remember

and let them know you're interested

Networking can be one of the most important things

business Building relationships plays a crucial role

the success of any business. Be positive about networking

attitude, smile and desire to build these relationships and

they happen. You will benefit more from the experience

you imagined

• Join and participate in forums in your field

Other members and who can see your forum replies

know that one day someone may ask to interview you or give a

to an agreement

You may not know what a forum is, but you might be

already participate in them. Sometimes they are called simply

message or bulletin boards, thread discussions, discussion

in forums or chat groups. When you participate in something

they are a forum.

The simple definition of a forum is a place where people can

start a conversation with threads and then reply

other people's threads. When one forum member writes

post, everyone in that community can see it. If you

If you want to reply to someone's comment, people can read it too

Your Answer. The conversation can evolve over time and everything else

Community members do not need to be online at

participate at the same time. You can decide for yourself whether you will participate in something

forum is enough or if it is necessary to participate in several forums.

They are a great way to receive as well as give wisdom from others

the voice of your business.

You can search for the forum in the navigation bars of your websites

favourite You can also simply search your forums

special niche. Some sites list many

all forums in one place. They will help you find them

which are best for you. You can join as many business forums as

you feel that depending on time and energy

put in them Don't forget that these are social arenas, but

conversations usually don't happen in real time. Simply tap a

lots of information and let others use yours.

Hosting a forum on your website can also be affordable. there

There are many reasons why forums are a good idea for your website.

1. They give your audience a place to be heard. They

can give their opinion about your website. you would be

amazed at how good ideas you get

improve your website. Of course, you will get many ideas

which are not big and even complaints but

the benefits may outweigh the negatives.

2. Forums can attract new people to your site. People love

to speak and express an opinion. If you give them a chance,

they do it. This attracts others to the site who want it

participate in the discussion.

3. They can level your content - if you get a lot

people in the conversation, your audience can

add content to your website for you. Forum posts are

content An active forum can add a lot of content and

because search engines like updated blogs

regularly, you can increase your chances of being seen searches

4. Humans are social by nature. We are looking for friends who

think like us and like to talk to them. If you do

the type of your site where people can do that and

meet new people and they will come back to you

to the website. This happens every time someone comes to your website

an opportunity to sell them something to keep them going

back is a good idea.

5. There is no reason not to get it. Forums are easy

and people enjoy them so not really

disadvantage for them.

The basic structure of the forum is simple. Every forum has

four parts. These are: the actual forum, classes,

topics and messages. Any forum you participate in or

you can have an unlimited number on your website

categories and/or subcategories. Classes are used to it

to master the subjects. When you go to the home page

in the forum you can see the list of categories and their number

topics in each category.

There are three main people involved in the forums:

1. Forum owners - These are the people who manage

forum They can change any forum level, create

discussion classes used for the forum, create

administrators and manage user groups.

2. Moderators - these are the people who moderate the classes

in the forum. They have the ability to delete messages

and/or topics or even ban people from participating forum

3. Users - These are individuals or members who have access

to the forum and registered there. Even though they didn't

any special rights, the forum owner can assign a

user as forum moderator.

One of the best ways to keep your audience interested in you

the site offers them access to an online chat

forum Forums are a great way to stay connected

clients and stay current in your field. They can be like that

you have a support network you can access 24/7.

You can also get the word out to your customers and/or

business partners 24/7. You can inform them about any news,

forum operations or future events. They will catch up

you send them all the links immediately and they don't have to wait

for email notifications.

You always want to stay in touch with your target audience. Forums are a great way to do this. The forum offers them a a place for questions and a place for you to answer. often

many people ask the same thing and all you have to do is

answer once Interaction is important. Creating your own clients

feeling that they are important to you can be a great advantage for you

business They also cover a large geographical area

it would not have been possible before.

Forums can be both entertaining and informative. Become a member

opening a forum is usually as easy as registering for it. Commitment

forum can give you an idea based on their years of experience

in your field. This can be invaluable for a new business. • Use social media to your advantage

Constantly posting on many social sites like Facebook,

Twitter, Google and LinkedIn are all great ways to add

content If you regularly post great tips, news and updates,

everything ultimately serves as content.

If you are not very social media savvy, you will have to spend money

on some of these sites. It will help you

you understand what the websites are talking about. Then you can start

align your business to the websites. It could be

valuable to your business.

Here are some tips to help you

world of social media:

1. Reply to all your Facebook comments

page is important - I know it can seem that way in your busy day like one more thing you have to do but it's worth it.

Visit your page at least once a day for a response

comments in time can really be made a

differential This helps people visiting your site get a

make a good impression on your company and they will

I appreciate your prompt action.

2. Use whatever background you like for your Twitter account

company - don't just click on the first one you come across. This

it might take a little longer to get it right, but it will work

is worth You want to give your audience a real feeling

who you are What distinguishes the most successful people

attention to detail is often in life. Take your time

change your account and it can do anything

difference in the world.

3. Familiarize yourself with your social media marketing methods

Competitors – Researching your competitors can help you

to get an idea of what works well in a particular niche. It can also give you an idea of what isn't working

and helps you know what you don't want to do. you

don't want to imitate your competitors. Take what you like

and put your own unique spin on it to make it your own.

As you develop your social media skills, you can

find new things you like and want to use. Social media

websites make it very easy to find innovative ways

things and express your business.

4. Make it easy to find people on sites like Twitter.

There are many blogging sites like Tweepi.com

makes it easy to find on Twitter. Tweet regularly

and automate your tweets so you don't forget them

who follow you

5. Don't just shove your product in - people tend to get up and

go to the bathroom during commercials. When they click on you

to see one giant ad, they click on it

secondly. What you want to do instead is offer

interesting content for viewers. You can use the content

that amuses them, educates them, or maybe even

inspire them. The "Share" button has been patched

your content spreads more easily. Even slightly viral

get your name out there. No one wants to share a

page of commercials. Engaging, educational, or

inspirational information, however, gets shared often.

Give your viewers what they want, and they'll pass it on to

others they feel will enjoy it.

6. Be original—No one wants to share something they've

seen 100 times on various sites. They want to share

unique things that evoke some kind of emotion or

a pleasant reaction to them. Therefore, you are more

succeed when you create new and interesting content. you

campaigns are found on social networks

successful See what content they share

with your viewers. It will help you create such content

people want to share on many different social media

network with all your friends.

7. The headline is often the first thing your audience sees.

They are usually in larger, bolder print and stand out on the page.

Learn how to create fun and engaging headlines for social media

media blogs. You will see many old titles,

got bored and hit the ground running. Good title though

can attract people to your page, blog or website. test

until you find what works for you.

8. Organize special offers or competitions

Facebook Page - Everyone wants to win something. This

it doesn't even have to be something big and expensive. All that matters is the thought of winning. to take

promotions or contests are one sure way to get yours

engaged followers. Maybe you want to offer a free product,

a small prize or even a coupon for a reduced price.

Whether it's big or small, it really doesn't matter much.

Don't get me wrong, millions of people will probably hit on you

would participate, if possible, to win a new car. it is

given You won't get as much with a 25% discount, but you can

get a lot Not only do you get them involved, they get involved too

convey to their friends who they know who they are

it may seem like they want to enter. You get a bigger audience,

and at the same time build goodwill with your customers.

It's the kind of thing where you really have nothing to lose

try It also builds goodwill with your customer base.

9. Not only the actual content is important, but also the format of the content

content can be important too - you get yours

attention of a follower if you post it in an easy-to-read format

to read the visual aspect of content can make it attractive

to your readers. This also makes them more applicable

Share it.

10. Use time off to your advantage - vacations

it's a good time to post content related to them. about

of course, it depends on what kind of business you have.

Maybe you want to post seasonal recipes, shopping tips

promotion or family relations. Mentioning the future

the holiday makes it interesting for the reader.

11. If you want more people to see your Twitter posts, use

hashtags - if you want to share cooking tips, e.g.

you can try #food or #cooking tags. it is

a great way to find people who normally don't follow you

listen to what you have to say and learn more about yourself.

Your posts will show up in more searches and get found

of more people.

12. Familiarize yourself with social media before you start using it

marketing - as in every stage of your business, only

it is not wise to jump without looking. Find a quality guide

shop that takes you through the social stages

before starting marketing

campaign A good guide covers all the different sites

and the benefits of each to help you choose

that work for you. It also tells the basics

How the pages are laid out is also important

strategies that improve your page quality and

increase traffic flow there. Building a business on social media is no longer realistic

option, it is necessary for the success of all businesses. There is no better

garden to plant seeds like social media. to like

when flowers grow, social media acts as pollination. plant seeds

and as they grow, your content moves through the winds of technology

for more people.

Know your "garden"

You can plant all the seeds you want in the desert, but that doesn't mean they grow the same applies to commercial seeds. Knowing your niche

to help you better prepare to plant the seeds to grow in it.

The most important part of this "garden" is the people in it.

1. Know the gardener - that means you! Know your business well.

It's impossible to know who likes you

business/products/services if you don't really know them.

Here are some things you should consider.

☐ Is what you offer designed to fulfil a need or

is this something considered a luxury?

☐ Are their others who offer what you sell? If so, what

makes your product unique and gives it an edge?

☐ See what your customers buy, who buys the most

of you and who spends the most money. Is it

what they all have in common

☐ Is your product/service designed to change your life

customers better or solve the problem for them? what is

benefit from what you have to offer?

2. Know those who visit, admire and buy from you

garden - this is your target market. You can never please everyone

people all the time, but knowing your target market

it means finding the right people. Then you can please

them

A "one size fits all" marketing strategy just doesn't work.

Every successful entrepreneur knows that it takes work

the right direction. For example, if you sell a mobile phone

accessories, you can't just assume they're wanted

anyone with a phone. There are many other factors involved

come join the game. The target market is so broad and

unfocused makes it impossible to focus on specific needs.

A successful campaign must know who it is targeting and why

target them This makes it much more efficient

campaign There are several things you can do to help yourself better

know and improve your market:

☐ See who benefits from you the most

must be offered. One way to do this is to pay attention to your own

social media sites. See what people are saying

you and what interests them most.

☐ Everyone has customers who are more difficult than

another Find these customers and ask them questions.

It can be on social media or even via email. ☐ Social media research can give you an opportunity

information and you can make it easy and fun

followers It gives you a lot of quality information about yourself

clientele

☐ Stay up to date with news and trends in your industry

with your competitors.

As you continue to research the market, you can begin to narrow it down

down and refine it further. If you do, it's even more things you should consider.

☐ What is the scope of the product? Do you sell regionally,

nationally or globally?

☐ Check Demographics:

1. Gender and Age - Is your audience predominantly female?

or a man? How much do they perform? Alignment a

can be a certain gender or a certain age group

of great importance. For example, there are not many of them

women's clothing should be aimed at professional men

to save A radio station that mainly uses rap music would be

I want to focus on a younger audience. This

it is usually quite easy to determine gender and age

for your product/service and it can be large

difference in your advertising campaign.

2. Income - Another demographic indicator is a person's income. If you're a discounter, you'll probably want to do this

target your products to the mid or lower tier

income class on the other hand, top fashion stores

target audience belonging to higher income group.

You want to target your product to those who have

income to buy it.

3. Lifestyle preferences - these are usually interrelated

about what a person likes, their hobbies or pastimes

interests They often serve special dietary needs, e.g

for diabetics or food allergies. someone

who sells swimwear wants to target those who

enjoy the water The target would be religious books

to those of that particular faith. Whatever

the lifestyle enjoyed by the target market focuses on it

your campaign.

4. Buying Cycles - Cycles in which you

Customers can also buy your products

important to target this market. For example,

you may have many people at lunch

a restaurant made up mostly of professionals

merchants Your dinner might though

mainly families with children. Because of that,

many restaurants make different menus

for each group. Chicken nuggets and fries

may not look very tasty from a professional, but from children there don't seem to be enough of them.

☐ Are your products aimed at other companies or

individual consumers?

You should now have a pretty clear picture of who you are

the specific purpose is. This will be the audience

receptive to your marketing strategy. You should develop your own

social media marketing campaign for these people.

3. Plant the seeds - now that you've narrowed down your target market

below, you know exactly where to plant the seeds for the best

result You will not waste your time and energy

too large an audience. You focus on a specific area

which earns you the most rewards.

That way you target your ad, not someone with a phone

certain phone owners. You're not trying to sell "hip" new phone cases

for professionals. You can target them to teenagers. you

not trying to sell simple neutral cases to teenagers. you know

where to direct your advertising campaign and save you

valuable time and money.

That way, you will also get much bigger rewards. you can do

smarter decisions about where to advertise and how to talk to you

Customers. You can advertise where your market thrives and

use language that speaks to them. Aligning your marketing strategy

you can satisfy your "customer".

It works the same if you are looking for someone to pay you

services Who want services? What bothers them the most? Like

How can I best promote the solution to them? However, make sure if you do

promises to your customers that you will follow through.

For example, you can promise fast working hours and get a lot

customers are knocking on your door. If you do not follow your

I promise, your whole campaign is useless. Just promote your stuff

can really offer to their customers. Think things like, "What I do is

better than anyone else?" How can what I do help solve my problem

Customers? Then promise them something you can give them.

You know your market and you know your message. The problem is now

where you put the message. How to choose the right tool

help you get your message across to your customers? In general, you want to use multiple advertising tools. In addition you can choose other things on social media. They are going

will vary depending on your audience. Your target audience decides

where you advertise. For example, if you advertise

a text message campaign to the younger generation may be the way to go,

because all young people love to text.

On the other hand, if you advertise to top corporate executives, they

it may seem like your text messages are heavy. For those who work

At the administrative level, posting dimensions usually work well and you can

your message to the intended audience.

Remember that sometimes different instruments and multiple touches are needed

Get your message across to your target market. Just don't assume it

the message will get there no matter where you deliver it. Appreciate everyone marketing channels and response mechanisms. It will help you

Choose the marketing medium that gives you the best response

on the market.

Just like a healthy garden requires good soil, proper watering and

fertilization, a good marketing campaign requires a defined and precise goal

a well-delivered message and the right medium to deliver it message

Taking care of your "garden".

You don't grow a garden by throwing dirt on a seed and expecting it to grow

to grow You appreciate it. The seeds you plant in your business also need care.

You can increase your customers in the following ways.

1. Networking, new client relationships - you spent hours at

seminars, exhibitions, workshops, etc. You talked to a lot of new ones

people, exchanged business cards and promised to keep in touch.

Cultivating that seed requires that you actually follow through on that promise.

Keep in touch with the people you meet and build relationships.

Relationships lead to satisfied customers. When you contact us

and then don't follow it, it's like throwing seeds to the wind.

2. Building a customer base - You have defined your goals

market and we have many new customers. A way to keep in touch

they must have a newsletter you can send them. Do that

potential customers can sign up and see your

the customer base is starting to grow. Ordering blog posts is another matter

do You spend hours preparing and posting brilliantly

content Allowing existing customers to subscribe to yours

messages, they receive them regularly. They can pass it on and

you will get more subscribers.

3. Use "calls to action" in your blogs - Give your audience a call to action

to do something Maybe you're talking about a great new product.

The call to action would be "click here_____ to view". Take them

Click the subscribe button to receive your blog regularly. Ask them to "share" it.

with a friend

4. Quality Content - This has been said many times in this book

for some reason - it is essential! Give your audience what they want

and you will see your customer audience grow.

5. Add links to your blog content - links can be too other

page on your website, social media page or even a page

belongs to someone else that you think your client will like.

Either way, you've given them content and it's helping them

build loyalty to you.

6. Promote your social media pages on your blog - this is great

a point that many companies miss. Encourage your readers

visit your social media pages and follow you on these networks

is another way to promote your content. This is the way to achieve

Customers. You can put social media buttons on your blog

for each of your social networks. That makes it easy

readers can follow you.

Growing a garden is one thing. However, making it bloom can be

secondly. Like any garden, different plants bloom at different times

in the year. You make your garden bloom by offering it to your customers

good service and quality information. You can do it because you are

to get to know them. You know who they are and what they need. Just like a gardener knows his garden and knows what it needs to grow.

You have a unique opportunity to provide your customers with a resource that is to meet their needs. If you meet these needs, there will be more

to you again and again.

Good customer service is a strong way to take care of your garden. Who the customer wants to feel special. If you know your customer well, then

you may want to develop a referral and reward system for them. when

a customer refers you, a special "thank you" with a discount

it can be a good incentive for the referring customer to even refermore

Conclusion

Growing a garden doesn't happen overnight. We all wish we could grow up

Our companies, like Jack, have grown the beanstalk. Just discard the seeds window and let this giant company grow overnight while we sleep. in

however, it doesn't work that way in reality.

Growing a business starts with planting seeds in the right place,

for the right people and to promote success. You can build good and strong

business step by step.

Whether you enjoy gardening or not, you know that growing crops takes a lot of work

a beautiful garden, but if you see it in full bloom every second

used was worth.

You may not need to do everything you need to. to grow your business

either. If you are not tech savvy, spend time socializing

Social media can seem like torture at first.

When you see what can happen from that hard work, that's it

the other is worth. You planted seeds that grew a

beautiful benefit garden. Then you can get these prizes.